core belief™

Bible Study Series
for senior high

WHY Forgiveness MATTERS

Group

Loveland, Colorado

Why Forgiveness Matters
Core Belief Bible Study Series

Copyright © 1997 Group Publishing, Inc.

Credits

Editor: Amy Simpson
Creative Development Editor: Paul Woods
Chief Creative Officer: Joani Schultz
Copy Editor: Pamela Shoup
Cover Art Director: Jeff A. Storm
Art Directors: Bill Fisher and Ray Tollison
Computer Graphic Artist: Ray Tollison
Photographer: Craig DeMartino
Production Manager: Gingar Kunkel

ISBN 0-7644-0887-9
10 9 8 7 6 5 4 3 2 1   06 05 04 03 02 01 00 99 98 97

Printed in the United States of America.

Bible Study Series
for senior high

contents:

the Core Belief: ▼ Sin and Forgiveness

To many of today's young people, "sin" is an outdated word. They have no understanding of absolute right or wrong because the culture around them has obscured these ideas. But absolutes remain—regardless of popular belief. Sin does exist, and that's why today's young people need to learn the lessons within this Core Christian Belief.

Sin is falling short of God's standard of perfection. Since Adam and Eve sinned by eating forbidden fruit, each of us has separated ourselves from God. We doom ourselves to physical and spiritual death by our disobedience. But God has bridged that gap through the death and resurrection of his Son, Jesus Christ. Because of this, God can forgive us and restore us to a relationship with him. We still sin, and he still forgives. And because he's forgiven us, he wants us to forgive others, too.

the ▼ Helpful Stuff

SIN AND FORGIVENESS AS A CORE CHRISTIAN BELIEF **7**
(or The Ultimate Problem)

ABOUT CORE BELIEF BIBLE STUDY SERIES **10**
(or How to Move Mountains in One Hour or Less)

WHY ACTIVE AND INTERACTIVE LEARNING WORKS WITH TEENAGERS **57**
(or How to Keep Your Kids Awake)

YOUR EVALUATION **63**
(or How You Can Edit Our Stuff Without Getting Paid)

the ▼ Studies

Dying to Live

15

THE ISSUE: Suicide

THE BIBLE CONNECTION: Matthew 26:47-50; 26:69-75; 27:1-5; and John 21:15-19

THE POINT: Forgiveness brings hope to life.

When Friends Fight

25

THE ISSUE: Friendship

THE BIBLE CONNECTION: 1 Samuel 18:1-16; 19:1-10; 24:1-22; and 26:1-25

THE POINT: Sin can destroy your relationships.

Violated

35

THE ISSUE: Sexual Abuse

THE BIBLE CONNECTION: Genesis 37:18-28; 50:15-21; Isaiah 55:7; and Luke 15:11-32

THE POINT: God can forgive anyone.

"I Was Wrong"

47

THE ISSUE: Repentance

THE BIBLE CONNECTION: 1 Samuel 13:2-14; Psalm 51:1-17; and Jonah 3:1-10

THE POINT: Admitting we're wrong helps us change our ways.

▼Sin and Forgiveness
as a Core Christian Belief

Today's young people have been desensitized to sin. They're bombarded by all kinds of sin in movies and television. Sex outside marriage is exciting and attractive—and often displayed graphically. To some kids, violence and killing are "fun" and acceptable. Ethics in business—or in daily life—are only for the weak or naive. Crime is profitable and reasonable—if you're smart enough to get away with it. And anyone standing up for Christian values or pure living comes off looking like a fool.

To young people, sin and its consequences can seem unreal—a used-up idea that's lost its merit in the flood of popular opinion. They see no need for God or the forgiveness he offers. Consequently, it shouldn't surprise us that few kids really take God seriously. Nevertheless, God's love for young people remains unchanged.

These lessons will help your kids develop a deeper understanding of what sin and forgiveness have to do with their lives. First, they'll explore the power of forgiveness. As they come to understand that forgiveness brings hope, they'll see that God has a better answer than **suicide.**

In the second study, kids will examine the power of sin. As kids delve into this hard-hitting topic, they'll discover that sin can destroy **friendships.**

Kids will then focus on the important and sensitive topic of **sexual abuse.** Through this study, kids will discover that forgiveness is a process and that God can forgive anyone—and help them to forgive.

The final study of this course directs kids to examine the meaning of **repentance** and discover its freeing power. Through this examination, kids can discover that although repentance may be difficult and unpopular, it can help them change their ways.

Understanding the reality and effects of sin can help your kids see their need for God's forgiveness. Only then can they appreciate the price Jesus paid to allow them the chance to know God and walk with him.

For a more comprehensive look at this Core Christian Belief, read Group's **Get Real: Making Core Christian Beliefs Relevant to Teenagers.**

DEPTH FINDER

HOW THE BIBLE DESCRIBES SIN AND FORGIVENESS

To help you effectively guide your kids toward this Core Christian Belief, use these overviews as a launching point for a more in-depth study of sin and forgiveness.

What the Bible Teaches About Sin and Forgiveness

- **Sin is essentially falling short of what God wants us to do.** We sin by doing things that don't please God, and we sin by not doing things that God wants us to do. Some picture it as missing the mark, like when you shoot an arrow at a target and don't hit it. Sin happens when we place ourselves above God by choosing to do what we want instead of what God wants (Deuteronomy 25:16; Ephesians 2:1-3; James 1:14-15; James 4:17; 1 John 3:4; and 1 John 5:17).

- **Adam and Eve introduced sin to humanity.** The sin they committed involved direct disobedience to one of God's commands. Prior to their sin, they didn't have the sinful nature we have. They were tempted by an outside source—the serpent, who was really Satan—and when they gave in to the temptation, sin permanently entered the human race. They chose to believe and obey the serpent rather than God, and all humans have been plagued by sin since that day (Genesis 3:1-13; Jeremiah 17:9; John 8:44; Romans 5:12; and 1 Corinthians 15:21-22).

- **All people in every age have sinned.** Because of the sin nature introduced by Adam and Eve, without God's help no human is able to refrain from sinning (1 Kings 8:46; Job 14:4; Ecclesiastes 7:20; Isaiah 53:6; Romans 3:10-12, 23; and 1 John 1:8).

- **Sin causes both physical and spiritual death.** God's standard is perfection, and with one single sin we've lost all possibility of being perfect. Therefore, we're cut off from God, and destined for spiritual and physical destruction. There's nothing we can do to wipe out our own sin and make ourselves good enough to have a relationship with God. We're totally at his mercy (Genesis 2:17; Isaiah 57:20-21; 59:2; Matthew 5:48; Romans 6:23; and Galatians 6:7-8).

- **God is ready to forgive anyone who seeks him.** Because of Jesus' death and resurrection, God can forgive our sins and restore our relationship with him. To receive God's forgiveness, we must confess our sin to him and turn away from the sin. When possible, we should make restitution for any wrong we've done against others. We must also be willing to forgive others who've wronged us if we want God to forgive us (Psalm 103:1-3; Matthew 5:23-24; 18:23-35; Luke 15:11-24; Colossians 1:13-14; and 1 John 1:9).

- **Though Christians try to please God, they still struggle with sin.** When we sin, we don't forfeit our relationship with God, but our fellowship with him is broken. Fortunately, forgiveness is readily available, and condemnation is nullified through the redeeming work of Jesus Christ in our lives (Romans 7:15-25; 8:1-2; Galatians 5:13-26; Ephesians 4:17–5:20; and 1 John 1:9).

- **God commands us to forgive others in the same way he has forgiven us.** God has made it clear that we're not to condemn others or seek revenge for the wrongs others commit. Instead, we're to turn the other cheek and forgive when we're wronged (Matthew 5:39; Matthew 18:21-22; Luke 17:3-4; Ephesians 4:32; and Colossians 3:13).

CORE CHRISTIAN BELIEF OVERVIEW

Here are the twenty-four Core Christian Belief categories that form the backbone of Core Belief Bible Study Series:

The Nature of God	Jesus Christ	The Holy Spirit
Humanity	Evil	Suffering
Creation	The Spiritual Realm	The Bible
Salvation	Spiritual Growth	Personal Character
God's Justice	Sin & Forgiveness	The Last Days
Love	The Church	Worship
Authority	Prayer	Family
Service	Relationships	Sharing Faith

Look for Group's Core Belief Bible Study Series books in these other Core Christian Beliefs!

about

core belief

Bible Study Series
for senior high

Think for a moment about your young people. When your students walk out of your youth program after they graduate from junior high or high school, what do you want them to know? What foundation do you want them to have so they can make wise choices?

You probably want them to know the essentials of the Christian faith. You want them to base everything they do on the foundational truths of Christianity. Are you meeting this goal?

If you have any doubt that your kids will walk into adulthood knowing and living by the tenets of the Christian faith, then you've picked up the right book. All the books in Group's Core Belief Bible Study Series encourage young people to discover the essentials of Christianity and to put those essentials into practice. Let us explain...

What Is Group's Core Belief Bible Study Series?

Group's Core Belief Bible Study Series is a biblically in-depth study series for junior high and senior high teenagers. This Bible study series utilizes four defining commitments to create each study. These "plumb lines" provide structure and continuity for every activity, study, project, and discussion. They are:

● **A Commitment to Biblical Depth**—Core Belief Bible Study Series is founded on the belief that kids not only *can* understand the deeper truths of the Bible but also *want* to understand them. Therefore, the activities and studies in this series strive to explain the "why" behind every truth we explore. That way, kids learn principles, not just rules.

● **A Commitment to Relevance**—Most kids aren't interested in abstract theories or doctrines about the universe. They want to know how to live successfully right now, today, in the heat of problems they can't ignore. Because of this, each study connects a real-life need with biblical principles that speak directly to that need. This study series finally bridges the gap between Bible truths and the real-world issues kids face.

● **A Commitment to Variety**—Today's young people have been raised in a sound bite world. They demand variety. For that reason, no two meetings in this study series are shaped exactly the same.

● **A Commitment to Active and Interactive Learning**—Active learning is learning by doing. Interactive learning simply takes active learning a step further by having kids teach each other what they've learned. It's a process that helps kids internalize and remember their discoveries.

For a more detailed description of these concepts, see the section titled "Why Active and Interactive Learning Works With Teenagers" beginning on page 57.

So how can you accomplish all this in a set of four easy-to-lead Bible studies? By weaving together various "power" elements to produce a fun experience that leaves kids challenged and encouraged.

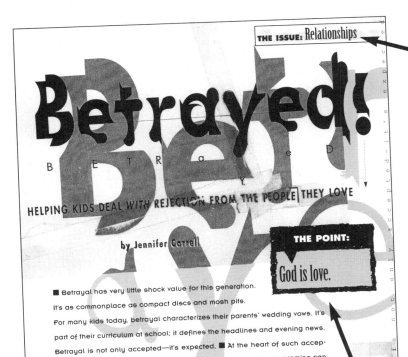

Betrayed!

HELPING KIDS DEAL WITH REJECTION FROM THE PEOPLE THEY LOVE

by Jennifer Carrell

THE POINT:

God is love.

■ Betrayal has very little shock value for this generation. It's as commonplace as compact discs and mosh pits. For many kids today, betrayal characterizes their parents' wedding vows. It's part of their curriculum at school; it defines the headlines and evening news. Betrayal is not only accepted—it's expected. ■ At the heart of such acceptance lies the belief that nothing is absolute. No vow, no law, no promise can be trusted. Relationships are betrayed at the earliest convenience. Repeatedly, kids see that something called "love" lasts just as long as it's [...] permanence. But deep inside, they hunger to see a [...]

The Study AT A GLANCE

SECTION	MINUTES	WHAT STUDENTS WILL DO	SUPPLIES
Discussion Starter	up to 5	JUMP-START—Identify some of the most common themes in today's movies.	Newsprint, marker
Investigation of Betrayal	12 to 15	REALITY CHECK—Form groups to compare anonymous, real-life stories of betrayal with experiences in their own lives.	"Profiles of Betrayal" handouts (p. 20), highlighter pens, newsprint, marker, tape
	3 to 5	WHO BETRAYED WHOM?—Guess the identities of the people profiled in the handouts.	Paper, tape, pen
Investigation of True Love	15 to 18	SOURCE WORK—Study and discuss God's definition of perfect love.	Bibles, newsprint, marker
	5 to 7	LOVE MESSAGES—Create unique ways to send a "message of love" to the victims of betrayal they've been studying.	Newsprint, markers, tape
Personal Application	10 to 15	SYMBOLIC LOVE—Give a partner a personal symbol of perfect love.	Paper lunch sack, pens, scissors, paper, catalogs

notes:

● **A Relevant Topic**—More than ever before, kids live in the now. What matters to them and what attracts their hearts is what's happening in their world at this moment. For this reason, every Core Belief Bible Study focuses on a particular hot topic that kids care about.

● **A Core Christian Belief**—Group's Core Belief Bible Study Series organizes the wealth of Christian truth and experience into twenty-four Core Christian Belief categories. These twenty-four headings act as umbrellas for a collection of detailed beliefs that define Christianity and set it apart from the world and every other religion. Each book in this series features one Core Christian Belief with lessons suited for junior high or senior high students.

"But," you ask, "won't my kids be bored talking about all these spiritual beliefs?" No way! As a youth leader, you know the value of using hot topics to connect with young people. Ultimately teenagers talk about issues because they're searching for meaning in their lives. They want to find the one equation that will make sense of all the confusing events happening around them. Each Core Belief Bible Study answers that need by connecting a hot topic with a powerful Christian principle. Kids walk away from the study with something more solid than just the shifting ebb and flow of their own opinions. They walk away with a deeper understanding of their Christian faith.

● **The Point**—This simple statement is designed to be the intersection between the Core Christian Belief and the hot topic. Everything in the study ultimately focuses on The Point so that kids study it and allow it time to sink into their hearts.

● **The Study at a Glance**—A quick look at this chart will tell you what kids will do, how long it will take them to do it, and what supplies you'll need to get it done.

The Bible Connection—This is the power base of each study. Whether it's just one verse or several chapters, The Bible Connection provides the vital link between kids' minds and their hearts. The content of each Core Belief Bible Study reflects the belief that the true power of God—the power to expose, heal, and change kids' lives—is contained in his Word.

THE POINT OF *BETRAYED!*:

God is love.

THE BIBLE CONNECTION

1 JOHN 4:7-21 The Apostle John explains the nature and definition of perfect love.

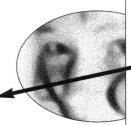

In this study, kids will compare the imperfect love defined in real-life stories of betrayal to God's definition of perfect love.

By making this comparison, kids can discover that God is love and therefore incapable of betraying them. Then they'll be able to recognize the incredible opportunity God offers to experience the only relationship worthy of their absolute trust.

Explore the verses in The Bible Connect mation in the Depthfinder boxes throughou understanding of how these Scriptures con

LEADER TIP for The Study

THE STUDY

DISCUSSION STARTER ▼

Jump-Start (up to 5 minutes) As kids arrive, ask them to thi common themes in movies, books, TV sho have kids each contribute ideas for a mass two other kids in the room and sharing their sider providing copies of People magazine to what's currently showing on television or at their suggestions, write their responses on ne **come up with a lot of great ideas. Even the ent, look through this list an try to disc ments most of these theme have in com

After kids make several suggestions, menti responses are connected with the idea of bet

● **Why do you think betrayal is such a**

Betrayed! 17

LEADER TIP for The Study
Because this topic can be so powerful and relevant to kids' lives, your group members may be tempted to get caught up in issues and lose sight of the deeper biblical principle found in The Point. Help your kids grasp The Point by guiding kids to focus on the biblical investigation and discussing how God's truth connects with reality in their lives.

DEPTHFINDER UNDERSTANDING INTEGRITY

Your students may not be entirely familiar with the meaning of integrity, especially as it might apply to God's character in the Trinity. Use these definitions (taken from Webster's II New Riverside Dictionary) and other information to help you guide kids toward a better understanding of how God maintains integrity through the three expressions of the Trinity.

Integrity: 1. Firm adherence to a code or standard of values. 2. The state of being unimpaired. 3. The quality or condition of being undivided.

Synonyms for integrity include probity, completeness, wholeness, soundness, and perfection.

Our word "integrity" comes from the Latin word *integritas*, which means soundness. *Integritas* is also the root of the word "integer," which means "whole or complete," as in a "whole" number.

The Hebrew word that's often translated "integrity" (for example, in Psalm 25:21 [NIV]) is *tam*. It means whole, perfect, sincere, and honest.

CREATIVE GOD-EXPLORATION ▼

Top Hats (18 to 20 minutes) Form three groups, with each trio member from the previous activity going to a different group. Give each group Bibles, paper, and pens, and assign each group a different hat God wears: Father, Son, or Holy Spirit. their goal is to write one list describing what God does in the

Depthfinder Boxes—These informative sidelights located throughout each study add insight into a particular passage, word, historical fact, or Christian doctrine. Depthfinder boxes also provide insight into teen culture, adolescent development, current events, and philosophy.

Leader Tips—These handy information boxes coach you through the study, offering helpful suggestions on everything from altering activities for different-sized groups to streamlining discussions to using effective discipline techniques.

Holy Profiles

Your assigned Bible passage describes how a particular person or group responded when confronted with God's holiness. Use the information in your passage to help your group discuss the questions below. Then use your flashlights to teach the other two groups what you discover.

■ Based on your passage, what does holiness look like?

■ What does holiness sound like?

■ When people see God's holiness, how does it affect them?

■ How is this response to God's holiness like humility?

■ Based on your passage, how would you describe humility?

■ Why is humility an appropriate human response to God's holiness?

■ Based on what you see in your passage, do you think you are a humble person? Why or why not?

■ What's one way you could develop humility in your life this week?

Permission to photocopy this handout from Group's Core Belief Bible Study Series granted for local church use
Copyright © Group Publishing, Inc., Box 481, Loveland, CO 80539.

Handouts—Most Core Belief Bible Studies include photocopiable handouts to use with your group. Handouts might take the form of a fun game, a lively discussion starter, or a challenging study page for kids to take home—anything to make your study more meaningful and effective.

Helpful Stuff   12

The Last Word on Core Belief Bible Studies

Soon after you begin to use Group's Core Belief Bible Study Series, you'll see signs of real growth in your group members. Your kids will gain a deeper understanding of the Bible and of their own Christian faith. They'll see more clearly how a relationship with Jesus affects their daily lives. And they'll grow closer to God.

But that's not all. You'll also see kids grow closer to one another.

That's because this series is founded on the principle that Christian faith grows best in the context of relationship. Each study uses a variety of interactive pairs and small groups and always includes discussion questions that promote deeper relationships. The friendships kids will build through this study series will enable them to grow *together* toward a deeper relationship with God.

Dying to LIVE
The Messages of Kids Who Kill Themselves

by Michael D. Warden

■ Thirteen teenagers will kill themselves today. ■ And tomorrow, thirteen more. And the next day, and the next. It adds up to around five thousand teenage suicides in a year. And for every "successful" suicide, there are at least a hundred other kids who attempt it and fail. ■ This may all seem like just numbers to you, but each number has a face—and a family, and friends, and a whole world of experience. Each number is a person, just like you. ■ This study focuses on the messages kids leave behind when they kill themselves—to discover why they self-destruct, and to help students reach for the true hope that God gives everyone who embraces his forgiveness.

THE POINT:

Forgiveness brings hope to life.

The Study
AT A GLANCE

SECTION	MINUTES	WHAT STUDENTS WILL DO	SUPPLIES
Relational Time	up to 5	GETTING TOGETHER—Talk about how they feel and what happened to them last week.	
Investigation 1	15 to 20	MESSAGES—Form groups to study different suicide letters, then teach each other what they learn.	"Final Notes" handouts (p. 23), paper, pencils, newsprint, markers
		WHY?—Discuss their findings and decide why young people kill themselves.	Newsprint list from "Messages" activity
Investigation 2	20 to 25	PARALLEL LIVES—Form groups to study different aspects of the lives of Judas Iscariot and Simon Peter, then teach each other what they learn.	"Lifeline" Depthfinder handouts (p. 21), Bibles, paper, pencils, newsprint, markers
		WHO'S LIKE WHO?—Discuss the similarities and differences between the kids they read about, Judas, Peter, and themselves.	
Reflections	up to 5	A LIGHT IN THE DARKNESS—Listen to a statement Peter made about Jesus later in his life.	Darkened room, Bible, candle, matches

notes:

Forgiveness brings hope to life.

THE BIBLE CONNECTION

MATTHEW 26:47-50; 27:1-5	Judas betrays Jesus in the Garden of Gethsemane, then later kills himself.
MATTHEW 26:69-75; JOHN 21:15-19	Peter betrays Jesus after his arrest, then later receives forgiveness from the resurrected Christ.

I n this study, kids will compare real-life suicides with the experiences of two of Christ's disciples: Judas Iscariot, who betrayed Jesus and then committed suicide, and Peter, who also betrayed Jesus but later received forgiveness for his betrayal.

By making this comparison, kids can come to understand how embracing forgiveness can be the key to hope and fulfillment in their lives.

Explore the verses in The Bible Connection, then study the information in the Depthfinder boxes throughout the study to gain a deeper understanding of how these Scriptures connect with your young people.

LEADER TIP for The Study

Because this topic can be so powerful and relevant to kids' lives, your group members may be tempted to get caught up in issues and lose sight of the deeper biblical principle found in The Point. Help your kids grasp The Point by guiding kids to focus on the biblical investigation and discussing how God's truth connects with reality in their lives.

THE STUDY

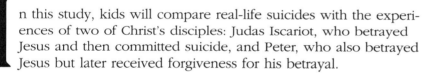

RELATIONAL TIME ▼

Getting Together (up to 5 minutes) As kids begin to gather in the meeting room, encourage them to spend time getting to know each other better. Ask them to tell about what's happened to them in the previous week or how they're feeling about their lives right now. If it's appropriate, pray together with kids who have special needs.

INVESTIGATION 1 ▼

Messages
(15 to 20 minutes)

After everyone has arrived and settled in, ask:

● **Who here knows someone who has talked about committing suicide or has actually attempted it?**

Ask some of the kids who raise their hands to briefly tell their stories to the rest of the class. Be certain kids don't use any names.

Once one or two stories have been told, say: **Why? What causes young people who are just beginning to tap their potential to throw it all away? Today our goal is to answer the question— What's at the heart of teenage suicide?**

Have kids form four groups (a group can be one person), and assign each group one letter from the "Final Notes" handout (p. 23). Explain to the groups that they're each to study their suicide note excerpt then follow the instructions for responding to what they read.

Say: **As all of you study the information I've provided, look for clues that might show root causes for why these young people committed suicide.**

Set out paper and pencils for groups to use. While kids are working, go around the room to help kids think through how they would respond to the person who wrote their assigned letter.

When groups are ready, have them each present their responses to the class. As each group reads its letters, jot down on newsprint any information they present that might point to why young people commit suicide.

Why?
Once all the groups have presented their information and all the clues are on the newsprint, ask:

● **Based on the information we've presented, what do you think pushes people to kill themselves?**

● **In a few of the suicide notes, some young people expressed guilt about their lives. What did they feel guilty about?**

● **Can you relate to the guilt these people felt? Why or why not?**

● **In what other ways do you identify with these people's lives?**

● **How do you deal with struggles like theirs in your life?**

Say: **One way we can work through the struggles in our lives is by talking to God about them and asking for his help. Turn to a partner right now, and tell about one struggle you're currently facing. Then pray together, telling God about your struggles and asking for his help. It's OK if you want to pray silently.**

When kids finish praying, continue by asking:

● **What's your reaction to the way these people chose to deal with their struggles?**

Say: **For all the reasons we've listed here, each of these young people lost hope in life. That was why they killed themselves. But it didn't have to be that way—for them or for any of you.**

Through the rest of our time together, we're going to discover how the true tragedy of the lives of these young people was that they never could allow themselves to embrace forgiveness— either for themselves or for others.

Understanding God's forgiveness could have saved these young people, because <u>forgiveness brings hope to life.</u> **God's forgiveness saves us all from death.**

"So Judas threw the money into the temple and left. Then he went away and hanged himself."

—Matthew 27:5

Parallel Lives (20 to 25 minutes)

Have kids form groups of six or fewer. Say: **We're going to go through another investigation of suicide, only this time you'll be studying the lives of two individuals from Jesus' day—Judas Iscariot and Simon Peter. As you go through this information, look for ways that Judas or Peter were like or unlike the young people you've already studied.**

Give each group a copy either of "Judas Iscariot's Lifeline" or "Simon Peter's Lifeline (p. 21)." Explain to kids that their goal is to learn their assigned information, then teach it to the other groups in a creative way that's never been done before. For example, kids might copy the information onto cards and tape them to their foreheads for other kids to study—anything goes!

Set out paper, pencils, newsprint, and markers for groups to use if they choose to. While kids are working, go around the room to help kids come up with creative, effective ways to convey their information to the rest of the class.

When groups are ready, have them each teach the rest of the class their information. As each group presents its information, jot down on newsprint any information they present that shows a similarity between Judas, Peter, and the suicide victims studied earlier.

LEADER TIP
for Who's Like Who

For the pair discussion, consider writing the questions on newsprint so kids can talk at their own pace.

Who's Like Who?

After all the information is presented and all the similarities are listed on the newsprint, ask:
● **Even though the lives of these people were all vastly different, what's one situation they've all had in common?**
● **Both Judas and Peter betrayed someone close to them. Do you think these other young people were betrayers? Why or why not?**

Have students quickly find partners. In their pairs, have them respond to these questions:
● **How are you a betrayer?**
● **How are you a forgiver?**
● **What's one positive quality about your partner that reminds you of God's forgiveness?**

Call everyone back together and ask:
● **As a result of the guilt and disillusionment they felt, both Judas and these other young people chose to kill themselves, and yet Peter did not. What was different about Peter?**

Say: **Judas and these other young people all did things or experienced things they couldn't live with. Their pride wouldn't allow them to forgive others or forgive themselves. But what's more important is that their pride wouldn't allow them to accept forgiveness from God either. So they passed judgment on themselves, and then carried out the sentence. <u>Forgiveness would've brought hope to their lives,</u> but they couldn't humble themselves to receive it.** Ask:
● **Why do you think Peter was able to experience God's forgiveness?**

DEPTH FINDER

JUDAS ISCARIOT'S LIFELINE

● His father, Simon, raised Judas in Kerioth, an area in the southern part of Judah (Joshua 15:21-25). All of the other disciples were from the north in Galilee.

● Read John 6:53-71. Many scholars believe that before joining the disciples, Judas was part of a violent group of Jewish nationalists who wanted to free Israel from Roman rule by bloodshed. Some conjecture that Judas may have followed Jesus in the hope that through him the nation of Israel would rise up against Rome and name Jesus as their new king. When it became clear this would not happen, Judas may have decided to betray him.

● Judas was appointed treasurer for the disciples (John 12:6; 13:29).

● Read John 12:1-6. When Jesus was anointed with expensive perfume at Bethany, Judas got angry at the "waste," pretending to be concerned for the needs of the poor. In fact, he was simply greedy.

● Read Matthew 26:47-50; 27:3-5. Judas sold Jesus into the hands of the Pharisees for 30 pieces of silver (the traditional price of a slave). At Jesus' arrest, Judas betrayed him with a kiss, then later felt remorse and threw down the money before the chief priests and elders. Not long after, he committed suicide.

SIMON PETER'S LIFELINE

● His father, John (also called Jona), raised Peter in Bethsaida, located in Galilee (John 1:42-44).

● Before Peter joined the disciples, he and his brother Andrew lived in Capernaum (Mark 1:21, 29) and worked as fishermen on the Sea of Galilee, along with Zebedee's sons, James and John (Luke 5:10).

● Read John 1:35-42. Peter probably came to follow Jesus through John the Baptist, who preached along the banks of the Jordan River. When Peter was personally introduced to Jesus by his brother Andrew, Jesus gave him the descriptive name Peter or petros, which means rock. The name became permanent. No other man in the New Testament bears that name. (See Matthew 16:18 and Mark 3:16.)

● After a period of companionship with Jesus during his early Judean ministry (John 1:42–4:43), Peter probably returned to his trade as a fisherman for a time.

● Read Luke 5:1-11. Later, when Jesus began his Galilean ministry, Peter joined Jesus full time, so that he could be trained (Mark 1:16-20). Peter went on to become the spokesman for all the disciples (John 6:66-69 and Matthew 16:16, 18).

● Read Matthew 26:69-75. After Jesus' arrest, Peter betrayed him by denying he ever knew Jesus at all.

● Read John 21:15-19. Later, after Jesus had risen from the dead, Peter received Christ's forgiveness for his betrayal.

DEPTH FINDER — UNDERSTANDING THE BIBLE

Second Chronicles 7:14 describes the process required for any person to receive God's forgiveness. This "heart progression" takes people from humility ("humble themselves")...to faith ("seek my face")...to repentance ("turn from their wicked ways")...to forgiveness ("then will I...forgive their sin")...and, finally, to hope ("heal their land").

● How can you experience God's forgiveness?
Say: <u>God's forgiveness brings hope to life,</u> but without it life becomes full of bitterness and disillusionment. We must learn to receive God's forgiveness. We must learn to forgive ourselves. And we must learn to forgive others.

REFLECTIONS ▼

LEADER TIP
for A Light in the Darkness

If your meeting room can't be darkened, take kids into a large closet for the closing. Or, if your group is large, consider giving them each a lit candle to hold and watch as you read the Scripture passage.

A Light in the Darkness (up to 5 minutes)

Darken the room, then light one candle. By candlelight, open your Bible to 1 Peter 2:22-25, then say: **Simon Peter went on to become a great light for the cause of Christ. Years after his betrayal, he wrote these words about Jesus...**

Have kids focus on the candle as you read the passage, then turn on the lights and say: **Pray for humility this week, so that you can experience <u>the light of hope that comes from God's great forgiveness.</u>**

Final Notes

What follows are real-life excerpts from various young people's suicide notes. After reading your assigned note, work as a group to write a short letter responding to your person's words.

Write your letter from one of these three perspectives:
- as if you were that person's best friend,
- as if you were his or her parent or sibling, or
- as if you were speaking for your entire generation of young people.

I must be one of those narcissists who only appreciate things when they're alone. I'm too sensitive. I need to be slightly numbed in order to regain the enthusiasm I had as a child. On our last three tours I've had a much better appreciation of all the people I've known personally and as fans of our music. But I still can't get out the frustration, the guilt and the empathy I have for everybody. There's good in all of us, and I simply love people too much, so much that it makes me too...sad.

Kurt Cobain, 27

Dear Mom and Dad,
I'm really sorry. I didn't want to hurt you, but I didn't know what else to do. Nobody really cares about me, and I can't live without someone who could love me. And you thought Ashleigh was just another girlfriend. (smile) Tell her I love her always and not to worry about me. I have notes to Princess and to Grady and Walter, too. Please be sure they get them. Maybe I'll see you someday. I'm scared!

— Michael, 18

DEAR WAYNE, IF I STAY HERE I'M JUST GOING TO BLOW MY BRAINS OUT, AND THAT WILL HURT EVERYBODY. BUT I CAN'T STAND TO KEEP LIVING THE WAY I AM NOW. SO I'M GOING TO RUN AWAY. AND HOPEFULLY SOMEWHERE, SOMEHOW, I WILL FIND HAPPINESS. AND IF I DO, I'LL COME HOME.

Paul, 17

You want to die when you're with me,
But I can't live without you, can't you see.
So, there is only one thing left for me to do
I have to do it to protect you.
Please understand, it's not your fault
I've felt this for awhile, and it's got to halt
But before I do, I'll give it one more try
But if it doesn't work then I'll say goodbye.
I am sorry to do it up there
But it's the only place I could figure where.
Because, you see I've had dreams too
But in them, this person doing this is me not you.
There is really nothing left here for me
And this is the way it has to be.
Please realize it's for the best
It really wasn't this problem it was all the rest.
The pressure just builds up and there's nothing to do.
Can't you see it's better to be me than you.
God I'll miss you.
Good-bye.

— Stacie, 16

When Friends fight

Why Friends Sometimes Become Enemies

by Siv M. Ricketts

Sin can destroy Your life.

THE POINT:

Sin can destroy your relationships.

■ Beep. Beep. Beeep! "We interrupt our regularly scheduled program in order to bring you this important message...Sin can destroy your life." ■ Not likely, right? ■ Yet every day the headlines are ablaze with tragedies that result from someone's sin—murder, suicide, abuse, car accidents caused by drunk drivers—the list goes on. ■ For today's teenagers, however, sin can be less obvious. Acting like a hidden infection, it worms its way into even their closest relationships, slowly consuming love and intimacy from the inside out. Kids may not realize why a friendship fails—but they definitely know it hurts. ■ This study focuses on the ways sin destroys relationships—and provides teenagers with positive tools for saving their friendships from the sin concealed within their own hearts.

The Study
AT A GLANCE

SECTION	MINUTES	WHAT STUDENTS WILL DO	SUPPLIES
Creative Investigation	10 to 15	SPEED CHARADES—Brainstorm characteristics that build or destroy friendships.	A watch with a second hand, paper, pencils, newsprint, a marker, prizes
Mock Trial	25 to 30	PEOPLE'S COURT—Hold a mock trial to examine the relationships between Saul, David, and Jonathan.	Bibles, newsprint, paper, pencils, markers, tape, magazines
Concluding Remarks	up to 10	BREAKING FREE—Share a specific failed relationship within pairs and pray together for forgiveness.	Bibles, construction paper strips, tape, pencils
	up to 5	VERDICTS—Create paper gavels and decorate them with verdicts that point out one "good friend" characteristic about their partners.	Paper, pencils

notes:

Sin can destroy your relationships.

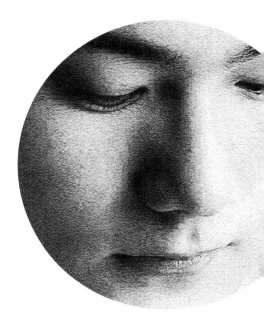

THE BIBLE CONNECTION

1 SAMUEL 18:1-16; 19:1-10; 24:1-22; AND 26:1-25   These passages describe the relationship between Saul, Jonathan, and David.

I n this study, kids will hold a mock trial to examine the relationship between Saul, David, and Jonathan—then glean from their example qualities that build up or tear down friendships.

Through this "trial," kids will discover how sin can destroy their own relationships and learn how forgiveness and love can repair sin's damaging effects.

Explore the verses in The Bible Connection, then study the information in the Depthfinder boxes throughout the meeting to gain a deeper understanding of how these Scriptures connect with your young people.

THE STUDY

LEADER TIP
for The Study

Because this topic can be so powerful and relevant to kids' lives, your group members may be tempted to get caught up in issues and lose sight of the deeper biblical principle found in The Point. Help your kids grasp The Point by guiding them to focus on the biblical investigation and discussing how God's truth connects with reality in their lives.

CREATIVE INVESTIGATION ▼

Speed Charades (10 to 15 minutes) Form two teams, and give each team paper and a pencil. Name one team the "Builders" and the other team the "Destroyers." Ask the Builders to brainstorm characteristics that build friendships (such as kindness or consideration), while the Destroyers brainstorm characteristics that tear down friendships (such as lying or gossiping). Tell teams they must each list at least eight characteristics, but the more they can list the better.

Once both teams have listed at least eight characteristics, explain the

DEPTHFINDER — UNDERSTANDING THESE KIDS

Some of your group members may be in relationships that have been so abused they seem almost impossible to repair. If this is so, it's important for kids to understand that, although God commands us to love and forgive everyone, he does not command us to be in a relationship with everyone. Friendship is a choice, and sometimes the best choice two people can make is to forgive each other for the hurts they've experienced and then let their friendship go.

game rules. Say: **On "go," the Builders have twenty seconds to work as a team to act out one of the characteristics on their list without talking. The object is to get the other team to correctly guess the characteristic. If the Destroyers guess correctly, they get a point, and vice versa. Teams will alternate turns. Both teams will win a prize if their combined scores add up to ten or more.**

(The prize can be as simple as a bag of M&M's candies or as elaborate as a coupon worth $2 off your next youth event.)

Write the characteristics and points scored on newsprint as the game is played. Afterward, ask:

● **If sin is any word, thought, or act against God's will, which of the characteristics you listed are sins?**

● **Is sin sometimes hard to identify? Why or why not?**

Have kids each turn to a partner to discuss these additional questions:

● **Which "friendship sin" do you struggle with the most? Explain.**

● **Do you think sin can ever build up a relationship? Why or why not?**

● **What's one positive friendship characteristic you notice about your partner? Explain.**

Say: **Sin can be subtle, but it's present in all of our lives. Today we're going to examine some relationships in the Bible to see how sin affected them and discover how <u>sin can destroy your relationships.</u>**

MOCK TRIAL ▼

People's Court (25 to 30 minutes)
Write these references on a sheet of newsprint so everyone can see them: 1 Samuel 18:1-16; 19:1-10; 24:1-22; and 26:1-25.

Say: **To help us take a closer look at the friendship among Saul, David, and Jonathan, let's transform this room into a courtroom, and hold a trial.**

Form three groups of Lawyers into "defense teams": one for Saul, one for David, and one for Jonathan. Then ask one person from each

DEPTHFINDER — UNDERSTANDING THE BIBLE

In Hebrew poetry, the numbers 10,000 and 1,000 were parallel. When in 1 Samuel 18:7, the women sang, "Saul has slain his thousands, and David his tens of thousands," they didn't literally mean that David had slain thousands more than Saul but that both were mighty warriors. That Saul was so incensed over the women's song is an indication of his own insecurity.

defense team to form a fourth group called the Jury. Once all the groups have formed, tell kids to creatively transform the meeting room to look like a courtroom. For example, kids might stack and arrange chairs to form the "bench," create a makeshift witness stand out of newsprint, or set up separate tables for each defense team.

Then say: **In this trial, each group has a specific task to fulfill. Defense teams, you must search the passages I've listed for evidence that shows how the loss of friendship between these three men was not your client's fault. Jury, your job is to read the passages I've listed to familiarize yourself with the case and make a decision of guilt based on evidence the defense teams present.**

Defense teams, once you have your evidence together, come up with a creative way to present it. You can write a group speech, act it out, draw pictures representing each piece of evidence— whatever your group thinks is the best way to convince the Jury of your client's innocence. Defense teams will take turns presenting their evidence, then the Jury will render a decision.

Set out markers, pencils, tape, magazines, newsprint, and paper for groups to use if they wish. Give the defense teams ten minutes to prepare their evidence, then call the court to order. As the leader, play the role of the Judge to direct the proceedings.

Once all the defense teams have presented their evidence, have the Jury render a guilty or not guilty verdict for each of the defendants— based on whether they believe that person's sin played a role in destroying his relationship with the other two.

When a verdict has been declared, have kids each find a partner to discuss these questions:

- **Why are friends important to you?**
- **What do you think went wrong with the friendships we've discussed among Saul, David, and Jonathan?**
- **How is that like what happens to friendships in your own life?**
- **When it comes to your own friendships, which person in the story are you most like? Explain.**
- **How does <u>sin destroy your friendships?</u>**
- **Based on what you've learned through this story, what can you do to stop sin from damaging your friendships?**

LEADER TIP for People's Court

The Jury members may finish the assigned reading before the other groups have gathered all their evidence. If they do, have them fill the time by discussing these questions within their group:

- Have you ever had to confront a friend because of a sin in your relationship? Explain.
- Have you ever lost a friend because of something one of you did to hurt the other? Explain.
- Why do you think we do things that hurt our friends?
- How can we avoid sin in our relationships?

LEADER TIP for People's Court

As the Lawyers are preparing their evidence, be available to help them organize their information as needed. Also, use the Depthfinders throughout the study to help kids more clearly understand the biblical passages.

LEADER TIP

for Breaking Free

It's possible that your students may have "friendship problems" with other people in class. Encourage kids to take time during this activity to get alone with their estranged friends and talk through their problems. (Rearrange the "pairs" to allow kids to do this.) Make yourself available to help kids through difficult issues, or pray together for God's forgiveness.

DEPTH FINDER   UNDERSTANDING THE BIBLE

If sin destroys, forgiveness rebuilds. In Matthew 6:14-15, Jesus says that if we don't forgive sins committed against us, God won't forgive us of the sins we commit.

Here are some other Bible passages that stress the power and importance of forgiveness: Matthew 18:21-35; Ephesians 4:31-32; and Colossians 3:12-14.

CONCLUDING REMARKS ▼

Breaking Free (up to 10 minutes) While kids are still with their partners, give every student a pencil and two strips of construction paper that are each long enough to fit around a wrist. Say: **Think of a specific failed or damaged friendship in your life, and write that person's initials on one of your strips. Write your own initials on the other strip.**

Distribute tape so that kids can use the construction paper to "handcuff" their wrists together. To create the handcuffs, have kids each tape a loop of construction paper around one wrist. Then have them each thread the other strip through the first loop and tape it around the other wrist. Encourage partners to help handcuff each other as needed.

When everyone is handcuffed, have partners discuss this question:

● **How is being handcuffed like having a damaged or failed relationship in your life?**

Say: **If you're willing, tell your partner about your failed friendship. Together try to figure out some of the sins that caused the relationship to fail. When you've finished, pray together that God would forgive you for any specific sin you committed in that friendship—and that he would help you be the kind of friend that he wants you to be.**

When students finish praying, have everyone stand. Read aloud Galatians 5:1. Then say: **As a symbol of Christ's forgiveness, break free from your handcuffs.**

"Saul was afraid of David, because the Lord was with David but had left Saul."
—1 Samuel 18:12

Verdicts (up to 5 minutes)

Have students turn back to their partners. Distribute paper and pencils, then say: **Choose one characteristic about your partner that makes him or her a good friend. For example, you might think that he's a good encourager or that she's a good listener. Then, tear your sheet of paper into the shape of a judge's gavel. On the "gavel," write your friendship "verdict" about that person, telling your partner what you appreciate about him or her. When you're both finished, exchange gavels.**

When pairs are finished, say: **Even though <u>sin can destroy your relationships,</u> you can be encouraged to know that the power of love and forgiveness is always greater than the power of sin.**

As you close the study, encourage kids to keep their gavels as a reminder to fight against the sin that can destroy their relationships.

Saul and David:
Anatomy of a Relationship Gone Wrong

What Happened	Where It's Written
God sends an evil spirit to afflict Saul, and David is brought to play the harp for him.	**1 Samuel 16:14-23**
David kills the giant Goliath and, as a result, Israel defeats the Philistines.	**1 Samuel 17:1-58**
Jonathan loves David. Saul becomes jealous of David's popularity with the people and tries to kill him.	**1 Samuel 18:1-16**
Saul offers David one of his daughters in marriage, thinking that will make David loyal. Instead, Saul sees that his daughter loves David and that God is with him, and he hates David all the more.	**1 Samuel 18:17-30**
Jonathan sees Saul's anger and warns David to hide so he'll be safe. Jonathan confronts Saul about trying to kill David.	**1 Samuel 19:1-10**
David flees to Samuel. Saul pursues him.	**1 Samuel 19:11-24**
Again, Jonathan goes to Saul on David's behalf, but Saul is furious. Jonathan warns David to flee for his life.	**1 Samuel 20:1-42**
Saul goes after David, who now has about 400 followers. Jonathan finds him and tells him that the Lord will keep him safe because he will be the next king.	**1 Samuel 21—23**
David doesn't kill Saul when he has the chance but confronts him, and they part ways.	**1 Samuel 24:1-22**
Saul again pursues David, and David has another chance to kill him but doesn't.	**1 Samuel 26:1-25**
Saul stops searching for David.	**1 Samuel 27:1-12**
Saul and Jonathan die while battling the Philistines.	**1 Samuel 31:1-13**

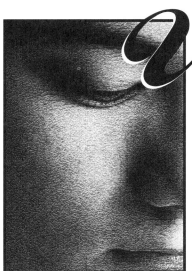

Violated

Dealing With Sexual Abuse

by Debbie Gowensmith and Helen Turnbull

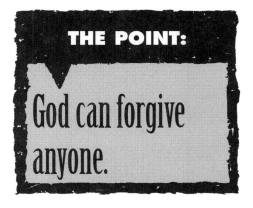

THE POINT:

God can forgive anyone.

■ Sometimes forgiveness is easy. A person makes a mistake that hurts you. The offender apologizes, and you forgive him or her. What's done is done. You move on. ■ But forgiveness isn't always that straightforward. ■ "[My neighbor] pleaded guilty to child molestation. He went to jail for two or three years. I wish he would've been in jail a hundred...There's no forgiving what he did, not at all" (Brian, quoted on an MTV special on sexual abuse, from America Online). ■ In cases like this, forgiveness isn't so easy. This kind of offender leaves scars that can last a lifetime—psychological, emotional, physical scars. And the offender may not even acknowledge that what he or she did was wrong. Can you forgive someone who does not ask for forgiveness? Are certain crimes so horrible that even God can't forgive them? ■ Because one of three girls and one of seven boys are sexually abused before they reach age eighteen (Ellen Bass and Laura Davis, *The Courage to Heal*), sexual abuse is not an issue we should be silent about. But this study cannot teach kids how to heal from deep wounds suffered as victims in any situation. It cannot provide a pat, pretty, fail-safe system on how to forgive and forget. Instead, this study can challenge kids to move beyond a superficial understanding of forgiveness. Kids will discuss how forgiveness might mean something different in various situations, and how forgiveness pertains specifically to victims of sexual abuse. And kids can discover that forgiveness is a long journey—one through which a God full of grace and love will help them.

The Study
AT A GLANCE

SECTION	MINUTES	WHAT STUDENTS WILL DO	SUPPLIES
Creative Introduction	10 to 15	FORGIVENESS FEUD—Play a game to uncover their attitudes toward forgiveness.	Bibles, index cards, pens or pencils, prizes or treats
Online Search	20 to 25	CHAT ROOM—Create a "chat room" to discuss sexual abuse, and explore Scripture to learn about forgiveness.	Bibles, chairs, pens or pencils, "NetTalk" hand-outs (p. 45)
Experiential Closure	15 to 20	FORGIVENESS TRAIL—Follow a masking tape trail while they learn that forgiveness is a process.	Masking tape, marker, newsprint, "Under-standing Forgiveness" Depthfinder (p. 43), pens or pencils

notes:

God can forgive anyone.

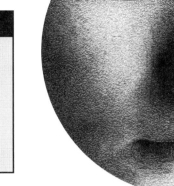

THE BIBLE CONNECTION

GENESIS 37:18-28; 50:15-21	Joseph's brothers sold him into slavery; he later forgave them for mistreating him.
ISAIAH 55:7	God promises to freely forgive those who come to him.
LUKE 15:11-32	Jesus used the parable of the prodigal son to teach about God's forgiveness.

I n this study, kids will explore others' struggles with forgiveness through a game show, a simulated "online chat," and Scripture, and they'll follow a trail to learn about the forgiveness process.

Through this experience, kids can learn that forgiveness can be a difficult journey. Kids can also discover that God can forgive anyone, and he can help them forgive, too.

Explore the verses in The Bible Connection; then examine the information in the Depthfinder boxes throughout the study to gain a deeper understanding of how these Scriptures connect with your young people.

LEADER TIP for The Study

Practice open communication by telling your students' parents that you'll be dealing with this sensitive topic. A good way to do this is to have a parent meeting a week or two before the study. Summarize the study, discuss the importance of talking about sexual abuse, and address parents' concerns.

BEFORE THE STUDY

For the "Chat Room" activity, make one photocopy of the "NetTalk" handout (p. 45) for every student. Cut apart the three messages.

For the "Forgiveness Trail" activity, use masking tape to create a trail in one area of your room. Start at one end of the room, and finish at the opposite end. In between, create a haphazard path that twists and crosses over itself. Use a marker to denote five points along the way, using a "1" for the first point, a "2" for the second, and so on. You can vary the distance between these five points, but make sure there's enough distance for a group of four to fit between numbers. Next create a corresponding sign for each point, using five pieces of newsprint and the "Understanding Forgiveness" Depthfinder (p. 43). On each piece of newsprint, write the step number boldly at the top and the corresponding explanation from the Depthfinder underneath the number. Finally, hang the pieces of newsprint in random order around the room, and place a pile of pens or pencils underneath each piece.

THE STUDY

CREATIVE INTRODUCTION ▼

LEADER TIP for Forgiveness Feud

If you have more than twenty-five students in your class, modify the game by using three teams for each round instead of two teams.

LEADER TIP for Forgiveness Feud

If you have a very small group, it's OK to have one person on a team, or you might want to eliminate the studio audience and play only one round.

Forgiveness Feud (10 to 15 minutes)

When kids have arrived, have them form two groups. Then have one group form two teams while the other group sits together on the floor as the "studio audience."

Say: **Let's start off today by playing a game. Our studio audience will have a very important role in the game today, and everyone will have a chance to be on a team and part of the audience. I'll briefly describe a situation to our first two teams, and then I'll ask them a question. Each team will have ten seconds to decide on an answer, write the answer on an index card, and bring the card to me.** Give each team three index cards and a pen or pencil, and ask each team to choose a team member to be the "runner." Then say: **While teams are deciding on their answers, each member of the studio audience will think about what his or her answer would be. After the teams have turned in their index cards, I'll read their answers to our audience. Audience, think about each answer carefully, decide which one is most like the answer you would have given, and then vote for that answer. The team that turned in the answer with the most audience votes gets a point. After three questions, the teams and the studio audience will switch places. Does everyone understand?** When everyone is clear on the rules of the game, say: **OK, teams, here's your first question: A boy accidentally steps on his dog's tail. The dog bites him. What does the boy do to the dog?**

"Let the wicked forsake his way and the evil man his thoughts. Let him turn to the Lord, and he will have mercy on him, and to our God, for he will freely pardon." — *Isaiah 55:7*

DEPTH FINDER RESOURCES

Following is a list of organizations and resources that are available to help people deal with sexual abuse.

ORGANIZATIONS

● Childhelp USA's National Child Abuse Hot Line, 1-800-4A-CHILD. The hotline TDD number for the hearing impaired is 1-800-2A-CHILD. This twenty-four-hour hot line can answer questions and direct callers to local help. Because it's a toll-free call, the number will not appear on your phone bill.

● Survivors of Incest Anonymous, a twelve-step recovery program for survivors of child sexual abuse. For more information, contact P.O. Box 21817, Baltimore, MD 21222, (410) 282-3400.

WRITTEN RESOURCES

● C.A.R.A.M.—Children Against Rape and Molestation—a magazine founded and written by teenagers for teenagers. For more information, contact P.O. Box 1293, Novato, CA 94948.

● *How Long Does It Hurt?*, a book for teenagers, their families, and friends about recovering from sexual abuse. By Cynthia L. Mather with Kristina E. Debye (Jossey-Bass, Inc., 1994).

LEADER TIP
for The Study

Because this topic can be so powerful and relevant to kids' lives, your group members may be tempted to get caught up in issues and lose sight of the deeper biblical principle found in The Point. Help your kids grasp The Point by guiding kids to focus on the biblical investigation and discussing how God's truth connects with reality in their lives.

After about ten seconds, ask the runner for each team to turn in the first index card. Shuffle the two cards, and then say: **Let's find out what our audience survey reveals.** Read both answers to the audience. Then read each answer again, and ask students to raise their hands to vote for the answer most like the answer they would have given. Remind the audience that each person must vote but may vote only once. Then say: Survey says..., say aloud the audience's choice, and award a point to the team with that answer. Continue this pattern with the next two questions:

● **Your best friend is invited to the most incredible party of the year, and you ask her if you can go with her. She tells you she's going with some new friends and you'll have to find some other castoffs to spend Friday night with. What do you say to your friend?**

● **Your cousin is killed in a car accident by a drunk driver, who is then sentenced to three years in prison. After the three-year term, you see the driver again. What do you tell him?**

Have the audience applaud for the teams. Then continue with the game by having the audience form two teams and the original teams sit down as the audience. Give three index cards and a pen or pencil to each new team, and have teams choose runners. Play the game as before, using these questions:

● **Your baby brother finds your favorite baseball card on the floor in your room and proceeds to chew the card to a soggy pulp. What do you do?**

● **Someone at school steals ten dollars from your locker. When you find out who did it, what do you say to her?**

● **Your friend confides to you that his older brother molested**

LEADER TIP
for The Study

Whenever groups discuss a list of questions, write the questions on newsprint and tape the newsprint to the wall so groups can discuss the questions at their own pace.

LEADER TIP
for Forgiveness Feud

It's OK if teams give vague answers or answers that don't have anything to do with forgiveness. Any answer will prompt discussion later.

him when he was little. The next time you see your friend's brother, what do you do?

Have the audience applaud for the teams; then give each person a prize or treat. Have kids form groups of five to discuss the following questions:

● **In our game show, were any questions harder to answer than the others? Why or why not?**

● **How did your responses vary with the different situations?**

● **What does it mean to forgive?**

● **How would you feel about forgiving the various wrongdoers from our game show situations? Why?**

● **What makes forgiveness easy or difficult?**

In their groups, have kids read Isaiah 55:7 and then discuss the following questions:

● **What does this verse say about forgiveness? about God's ability to forgive?**

● **Do you think God's ability to forgive varies from situation to situation? Why or why not?**

● **Do you think God can forgive anyone for anything?**

Say: **For us, forgiving someone may be an easy task or a difficult task, depending on the situation. But with Jesus, God promises not only to forgive us but also to forget our sin. God can forgive anyone, but sometimes we need his help to forgive people who hurt us. Let's explore this issue further.**

ONLINE SEARCH ▼

LEADER TIP for Chat Room

If you choose to modify this activity in any way, be sure to retain the elements of anonymity and separateness. Because the issue of sexual abuse is so personal and possibly emotional, kids need to process the information with at least some privacy. They also need to feel the protection anonymity provides.

Chat Room (20 to 25 minutes) Line up two rows of chairs back to back in the middle of the room. Have students sit in the chairs, and distribute pens or pencils. Say: **Sometimes talking with other people on the Internet feels comfortable because we can join in conversations anonymously. We're going to create our own "chat room" to talk more about forgiveness. First, to get into the chat room, everyone will need to make up a "screen name."** Give students a few seconds to create pseudonyms they can use to sign their responses. Encourage kids to use screen names that they haven't used before and that won't identify them.

After kids have created screen names, say: **Now let's go "online." I'm not going to ask you to reveal personal information, and you don't have to say or do anything you don't want to. When you receive the first message, read it and write a response. Write the response with the hand you don't normally write with or disguise your handwriting some other way so you retain your chatroom anonymity. Here's the first message.**

Give each student a copy of Message 1 from the "NetTalk" handout (p. 45), and give the students one minute to read it and respond by writing on the handout with the hand they don't normally write with. When kids are finished writing, say: **Now you're going to send your message. Sign your screen name, fold the paper in half, and pass**

DEPTH FINDER
UNDERSTANDING YOUR ROLE

Here are some symptoms that may indicate that a teenager is struggling with a major problem like sexual abuse:

- extreme fear or intense anger without an obvious cause
- inability to trust others or unwillingness to participate in group activities
- a decline in school performance or a shift in friendships
- recent and radical changes in personality, such as depression
- problems sleeping, eating disorders, unusual fantasies
- inappropriate sexual behavior, promiscuity, or bizarre sexual knowledge
- presence of sexually transmitted diseases
- self-destructive behaviors such as burning or cutting oneself, running away, drug or alcohol abuse, suicide attempts

Once you suspect that a teenager may be a victim of sexual abuse, what can you do? Unless someone confides in you about abuse, don't ask direct or leading questions about abuse. Doing so may cause a person to falsely claim that he or she has been abused. Ask questions without leading or prompting kids toward answers (Marilyn Elias, "Suggestive questions can induce kids to falsely claim abuse," USA Today, August 13, 1996). For example, ask questions about behavior changes: "In the past few weeks, you've been withdrawn, and you seem depressed. I'm beginning to wonder if more is going on than just growing pains."

If the person acknowledges the changes, ask gently about the cause. If the person is completely resistant, don't push. Encourage the person to talk with someone he or she trusts. If the teenager seems hesitant but says he or she would like to talk, cite the protection, support, and hope that you and the church can offer.

If a teenager confides that he or she is being or has been abused, what should you do? Listen carefully and sensitively. Instead of interrupting or offering advice, let the teenager talk freely. Ask gentle questions that allow the person to control the conversation, such as "Do you think you can talk about that?" or "How did that make you feel?" Don't ask the person to reveal more than he or she wants to; don't suggest that the person encouraged the abuse; and don't excuse the offender in any way. It's important to believe the teenager even when accusations seem impossible, but also to be cautious about making unfounded accusations if a person might be lying.

How can you help in the healing process? Support the teenager and the family, and provide spiritual guidance. *Be aware that you have a legal responsibility to report abuse.* Contact your local or state child protection agency to learn about the laws in your area. Your role is not to investigate claims or provide counseling. Help the student find a trusted professional counselor.

During the teenager's long, painful healing process, use these suggestions to create a safe, loving environment:

- Affirm the person frequently and sincerely. Praise his or her inner strengths and qualities instead of outward appearance.
- Guide the person to turn to God for healing and strength.
- Support the teenager through his or her fear, grief, and other emotions.
- Pray daily for the person, and pray with him or her often.
- Help the teenager understand that healing will take time.

(Unless otherwise noted, information in the Depthfinder is compiled from *Josh McDowell's Handbook on Counseling Youth* by Josh McDowell and Bob Hostetler; *Counseling Helpsheets* by Tom Klaus and G. Lamar Roth; and "Sexually Abused Kids: How to Unearth the Truth and What You Can Do About It," by Dan Allender, Group magazine, February 1995.)

LEADER TIP

for Chat Room

You can add variety to this activity by having kids switch directions as they pass their messages or pass their messages overhead to the people behind them. Be sure kids pass their messages quickly and frequently so they can't figure out who the messages they receive came from. Also, be sure all kids have the same color ink or lead to write with so their writing won't be identified.

it to your left until I say "stop."

After about fifteen seconds, have each student stop, open the message, read it, and add a response. Remind kids to continue writing with the hands they don't normally write with and signing their screen names to their responses. Have kids send the messages again by folding and passing the papers. Then say: **Wait! Another message is coming over the Net.**

Distribute Message 2 to students, and have kids continue to write responses and send them. Repeat the process with the third message. Each message should circulate to at least three students, but you can have kids circulate them more if time allows.

Once kids have finished circulating the third message, have them form groups of four. Give each person a Bible, and have groups read Genesis 37:18-28; 50:15-21; and Luke 15:11-32.

After a few minutes, have groups discuss these questions:

● **How were the victims in these passages like the victim of sexual abuse we talked to online? How were they different?**

● **Do you think Joseph and the father in the parable found it easy to forgive?**

● **Do you think a victim of sexual abuse can or should forgive the offender? Why or why not?**

● **What are the advantages to forgiving someone? the disadvantages?**

● **In these Scripture passages, how did God treat the victims? the offenders?**

● **What were the consequences of the offenders' sins?**

● **Do you think forgiving an offender relieves him or her of the sin's consequences?**

● **Do you think God forgave the offenders in these stories? Explain.**

● **Do you think God can forgive a sexual abuser?**

● **Do you think God can help us to forgive? How?**

Say: <u>**God can forgive anyone,**</u> and God wants us to forgive others, too. With God's help, the process of forgiveness can be easier. But it is still a process—sometimes a long, difficult, painful process. Sometimes, as in cases of sexual abuse, it requires deep healing first.

EXPERIENTIAL CLOSURE ▼

Forgiveness Trail (15 to 20 minutes)
Have kids gather in the area where you put the masking tape trail. Say: **This masking tape line represents the process of forgiveness; as you can see, it's very complicated. Get into groups of four so you'll have some support. Each of you think about a situation in which someone needs forgiveness. You can think of your own situation, you can use the sexual abuse situation we read about in our chat room, or you can use a situation**

DEPTHFINDER
UNDERSTANDING FORGIVENESS

True forgiveness involves a sense of moral love; the victim sees the offender as a human being—flawed, but worthwhile because he or she is a human being. This type of forgiveness is separate from the victim's fear or anxiety. It isn't motivated by manipulative goals, condescension, or hostility. Instead, the victim's attitudes and feelings toward the offender change.

To help your kids further understand how the process of forgiveness can work, use the steps below for the "Forgiveness Trail" activity.

1. In prayer, ask God to help you heal and forgive.

2. Confront the anger and resentment you feel; find a healthy way to release the anger.

3. View the offender as a human being, not a stereotype; identify with—not excuse—the offender to gain compassion.

4. Recognize that you need forgiveness sometimes and that Jesus forgives the offender.

5. Allow an internal, emotional release of pain and anger.

(Information in this Depthfinder adapted from Suzanne Freedman et al., "Five Points on the Construct of Forgiveness Within Psychotherapy," *Psychotherapy,* Fall 1991; and Michael E. McCullough and Everett L. Worthington, Jr., "Models of Interpersonal Forgiveness and Their Applications to Counseling: Review and Critique," *Counseling and Values,* October 1994.)

from our game show. With your group, think of a creative way to travel together. The only rule is that you have to all be connected—linking elbows, in a single file line with everyone hanging onto the person in front of him or her, or two people riding piggyback, for example. In your group, follow the masking tape line until you reach a number written on the tape. Then find the piece of newsprint hanging on the wall that corresponds to that number. Still with your group, go to the newsprint, read it, and write a sentence reflecting what that step would be like in the situation you're thinking of. When everyone in your group is finished writing, go back together to the trail and continue until you get to the next number. Continue with this process until the end of the line. Is everyone ready?**

Have kids line up with their groups; then say: **When we're on the trail of forgiveness, we may feel alone. The process can be long and difficult, but God is always with us. Let's begin the process with prayer.** Pray aloud: **Dear God, we know that** <u>you can forgive anyone.</u> **It's hard for us sometimes to be forgiving. Please help as we struggle to forgive those who have hurt us. Thank you for your loving grace and your strength. Amen.**

Send the first group of kids on the trail. As soon as a group has finished at the first station, send a new group. After every group has finished, have everyone cheer their success and then turn to each of their group members and tell them how they helped them through the process. Then have the whole class discuss the following questions:

● What was it like to start the forgiveness trail by asking for God's help?

● What did you like or dislike about having people travel with you?

● What was the hardest stage? the easiest?

● Do you think God forgives in the same way we forgive?

Say: God is infinitely wiser than we are. He loves us completely and extended the ultimate in grace to his people through Jesus Christ. <u>God can forgive anyone.</u> Although his forgiveness doesn't require this long and intense process, he can be your guide as you go through the process.

NetTalk

Message 1

Sexual abuse is when someone, for his or her own pleasure, has sexual contact or conversation with a child. One out of three girls, and one out of seven boys, are sexually abused by the time they reach the age of eighteen.

Whoa! Those are powerful stats. I can't believe it affects so many people! How do you feel about this info? Do you think it's for real? —Phatso

Message 2

A man very close to my family started sexually abusing me as a toddler, and while I've forgotten some details of the encounters, I've never forgotten the pain. Every time I looked in the mirror, I saw someone who I couldn't love—someone I downright hated. No matter how hard I tried, I couldn't get rid of the shame. Not with booze, or sex, or drugs. I remember all my life thinking, "I wish I was dead. I wish I was dead." How could I ever forgive him? What would you do if you were me? —Songbird

Message 3

The problem was I confused forgiving the offender with liking him. I realize now that I can forgive him without liking him. I found out later the offender was also sexually abused as a child, and it made me realize that he is human. The healing and forgiving process began when I realized I am never alone. Healing is having the Lord reveal himself to you, and I think that's a lifetime process. What are your thoughts? Do you agree, or do you think I should forget about forgiving him? —Songbird

(Songbird's story adapted from the story of singer Julie Miller by Mark Moring, "Desperate for Love," Campus Life, April 1996.)

"I Was Wrong"

Helping Kids Experience the Freeing Power of Repentance
by Bob Buller

THE POINT:

Admitting we're wrong helps us change our ways.

■ "I didn't do it!" ■ "I get blamed for everything!" ■ "I didn't do anything wrong!" ■ "It's not my fault!" ■ Admitting that we've done something wrong doesn't come easy. In fact, admitting that we're wrong is so painful that most of the time we use these (and other) defenses to try to prove our innocence. ■ The easiest defense is simply to deny any involvement: "You're accusing the wrong person. Someone else did it!" This approach is especially effective, or so it seems, when we follow it up with the standard appeal for pity. "You blame me for everything—even when I haven't done anything wrong!" ■ Of course, if we've been caught red-handed, we take a different tack. We argue that our actions have been misunderstood, that there was nothing wrong with what we did. "Sure, I did it, but there's nothing wrong with what I did." Or perhaps we attempt to shift the blame to someone else: a sibling, an enemy, or society at large. "You can't blame me because someone else *made* me do it." And so the game of avoiding blame goes on and on and on. ■ Common as they are, these defenses simply don't work with God. God knows when we've done something wrong, and the only words he wants to hear at that time are "I was wrong." God wants all of us, teenagers and adults, to admit our sins, to honestly confess when we've done something wrong, because that's the only way we'll ever be able to change our ways. ■ This study will help your kids learn what repentance is all about and why it is so vital to spiritual and personal growth. In so doing, it will enable your kids not only to face their own shortcomings, but also to overcome the sins with which they so often struggle.

it's not my fault!

The Study
AT A GLANCE

SECTION	MINUTES	WHAT STUDENTS WILL DO	SUPPLIES
Opening Experience	15 to 20	BEATING THE RAP—Try to defend themselves against a "crime" they committed, and tie themselves together if they're found guilty.	"Facts of the Case" handouts (p. 56), pencils, paper, strips of ribbon or narrow cloth
Personal Reflection	10 to 15	SIN SAFARI—Cover a sheet of newsprint with sins common to teenagers, then secretly list the sin with which they struggle most.	Paper, pencils, newsprint, tape, marker, index cards
Biblical Examination	15 to 20	THE KEY TO FREEDOM—Study negative and positive examples of repentance in the Bible, then creatively teach each other what they learn.	Bibles, copies of the "Biblical Repentance" Depthfinder (p. 53), markers, newsprint, tape
Closing Application	up to 10	BREAKING THE BONDS—Apply what they've learned by silently confessing their sins to God and then cutting themselves free from their group members.	Bible, index cards from "Sin Safari" activity, markers or pencils, scissors

notes:

Admitting we're wrong helps us change our ways.

THE BIBLE CONNECTION

1 SAMUEL 13:2-14	Samuel announces that God will punish Saul for offering a sinful sacrifice and blaming his sin on others.
PSALM 51:1-17	David confesses his sin, commits to change his ways, and asks God to help him keep his commitment.
JONAH 3:1-10	Jonah warns of God's judgment, so the Ninevites repent of their evil ways.

I n this study, kids will act as their own "attorneys," trying to defend themselves for a crime they committed. Then they'll discuss how they defend themselves when they sin in real life. Kids will also identify sins they struggle to overcome and discuss why these sins have such a hold on their lives. Finally, kids will discover from God's Word why they need to confess their sins to God instead of denying them or trying to explain them away.

By studying the biblical view of repentance, kids will learn that repentance involves more than just saying they're sorry; that admitting their sins will help them change their ways. As a result, kids will be challenged to take the first step in overcoming sins they struggle with by confessing those sins to God and by committing to change their ways.

Explore the verses in The Bible Connection, then examine the information in the Depthfinder boxes throughout the study to gain a deeper understanding of how these Scriptures connect with your young people.

BEFORE THE STUDY

For "Beating the Rap," photocopy the "Facts of the Case" handout (p. 56). You'll need one copy for every four students.

For "The Key to Freedom," make one photocopy of the "Biblical Repentance" Depthfinder (p. 53) for every eight students. Then cut apart the two sections of the Depthfinder. You'll need one section for every four students.

LEADER TIP for The Study

Because this topic can be so powerful and relevant to kids' lives, your group members may be tempted to get caught up in issues and lose sight of the deeper biblical principle found in The Point. Help your kids grasp The Point by guiding kids to focus on the biblical investigation and discussing how God's truth connects with reality in their lives.

THE STUDY

OPENING EXPERIENCE ▼

LEADER TIP
for Beating the Rap

To prevent injuries, make sure kids don't tie themselves together too tightly. In addition, be sure you have several pairs of scissors handy in case kids need to evacuate the room or the building in a hurry.

Beating the Rap (15 to 20 minutes)

Have kids form "defense teams" of four kids each. Give each defense team a copy of the "Facts of the Case" handout (p. 56) and a pencil. Then tell kids they have five minutes to prepare their defense against the charges and evidence described on the handout. Although they actually committed this crime, they are to devise any strategy they can to refute, call into question, or explain away the evidence. Each team will have one minute to present its defense.

Allow teams five minutes to think up their defenses, then ask team representatives to present their teams' defenses. While each representative is talking, listen carefully and jot down notes on a sheet of paper.

When all the teams have presented their defenses, announce a verdict for each team. If any groups simply admitted they were wrong, promised not to commit the crime again, and threw themselves on the mercy of the court, declare those groups guilty but promise to help them change their ways. Declare all other teams guilty, explaining that they didn't present acceptable defenses. Then give each member of those teams a ribbon or a strip of narrow cloth, and instruct team members to tie their ankles or wrists together with the cloth. Announce that team members will remain tied together until the end of the study.

Then have team members discuss the following questions. After each question, ask volunteers to report their teams' answers. Ask:

● **What was the easiest part of preparing your defense? What was the hardest?**

● **What are some ways we defend ourselves when we're wrong in real life?**

● **What did you like about defending yourself when you knew you were wrong?**

● **How is this like the way you react to sin in real life? How is it different?**

● **How does defending yourself when you're wrong "tie you up" in real life?**

Then say: **Your dream defense teams may have beaten the rap in a real court of law, but you're dreaming if you believe you can fool God into thinking you're innocent when you're not. In fact, there's only one way for us to avoid being tied up by sin and its consequences. So today we're going to discuss how <u>admitting we're wrong helps us change our ways.</u>**

DEPTHFINDER
UNDERSTANDING YOUR KIDS

The kids in your group no doubt struggle with many, if not all, of the same sins that other teenagers (and adults) grapple with: lying, lust, gossip, selfishness, hatred, cruelty, laziness, materialism, jealousy, greed, envy, arrogance, rebellion, meanness—the list could go on and on. Moreover, if your kids are like other church-attending teenagers, five out of every ten of them have cheated on a test or exam, one out of ten has used alcohol within the past thirty days, one out of ten has tried marijuana, and three out of ten have engaged in sexual intercourse. Help your kids begin to overcome the sins that plague and enslave them by introducing them to the freeing power of true repentance.

(Sources for statistics: *America's Youth in the 1990s*, Robert Bezilla, editor; and *Josh McDowell's Handbook on Counseling Youth* by Josh McDowell and Bob Hostetler.)

PERSONAL REFLECTION ▼

Sin Safari · (10 to 15 minutes)

Keep kids in their groups of four. Give each group a sheet of paper and a pencil. Then challenge groups to list all the sins they can that kids their age struggle with. Explain that groups have two minutes to fill their sheets with sins.

While groups are working, hang a sheet of newsprint. After two minutes, have groups take turns reporting one sin at a time. Write each sin on the newsprint. Continue until every group has reported all the sins it listed. If you haven't covered the newsprint with sins, challenge kids to call out additional sins until the entire newsprint is covered with sins.

Then ask the entire group the following questions:

● **How difficult was it to think of sins that kids your age struggle with?**

● **How might the list change if we listed sins this group struggles with?**

● **What does this imply about how widespread sin is? how powerful it is?**

● **Why do you think kids your age struggle with so many different sins?**

Give each person an index card and a pencil. (If you have markers available, let kids use them to draw their symbols.) Instruct each person to think of the one sin he or she struggles with most. It can be a sin listed on the newsprint or some other sin the person didn't want to mention earlier.

Allow a minute of think time, then have each student draw a symbol to represent that sin on his or her index card. When kids finish their cards, direct them to fold them in half so the symbols are hidden, but to keep their cards for use later in the study.

When everyone has finished his or her card, have kids discuss the following questions in their small groups. After each question, ask volunteers to report their groups' answers. Ask:

● **How difficult was it to admit that you struggle with that sin?**

LEADER TIP for Sin Safari

Encourage kids to respect each other's privacy as much as possible as they draw. Of course, this will be a little difficult for kids tied to one another, but use this teachable moment to remind kids how difficult it is to hide our sins from others and from God in real life.

● **How do you feel about yourself whenever you commit that sin?**

● **How do you think God feels about you whenever you commit it?**

● **Why is it so hard for you to stop doing what you know is wrong?**

● **How would your life be better if you could overcome that sin?**

Then say: **Sin is one of the strongest forces known to humanity. In fact, sin sometimes gets such a grip on our lives that, even when we know what we're doing is wrong, we're powerless to stop it. But God is stronger than any sin, and he wants to help free us from our sins. So let's discover what God's Word says about how admitting we're wrong helps us change our ways.**

BIBLICAL EXAMINATION ▼

The Key to Freedom
(15 to 20 minutes)

Assign half the groups 1 Samuel 13:2-14 and the other half Jonah 3:1-10. Give groups copies of the appropriate sections of the "Biblical Repentance" Depthfinder (p. 53). Then direct groups to read their passages and sections of the Depthfinder.

While kids are reading, write the following questions on a sheet of newsprint and hang it where everyone can see it:

● What sins were mentioned in your Scripture?

● How did the person(s) sinning react to the sin?

● How did God respond to the person(s) sinning?

When groups finish reading, tell them they have three minutes to answer the questions on the newsprint. Give each group a pencil, and encourage groups to record their answers on the back of their Depthfinder handouts because they'll be teaching the rest of the group what they learn.

After three minutes, challenge each group to think up a creative way to teach the other groups what they learned from their passages. For example, groups might act out what happened in a play or opera, turn the story into a poem, draw on newsprint a series of cartoons that tell the story, or create a newscast describing the events of the passage. Tell groups they have five minutes to think up and create their lessons.

When time is up, have groups take turns presenting their lessons to everyone else. Encourage kids to applaud each effort. When every group has presented, have kids discuss the following questions in their small groups:

● **Which was worse: Saul's sin or the Ninevites' sins? Explain.**

● **What do you think God should've done to Saul? the Ninevites?**

● **Why do you think God punished Saul? forgave the Ninevites?**

● **What do these passages teach about how God feels about sin?**

● **What do they reveal about what God is most concerned with?**

When groups finish their discussions, ask volunteers to report the groups' answers to each question. Then say: **God is more concerned with our response to sin than with the "size" of the sins we commit.**

DEPTHFINDER · BIBLICAL REPENTANCE

Saul

Some time prior to the incident recorded in this story, God had told the prophet Samuel to designate Saul as Israel's first king (1 Samuel 9:1–10:3). To prove that Saul was his choice for king, God had even given Saul the ability to prophesy (1 Samuel 10:4-13) and victory over Israel's enemies (1 Samuel 11:1-11). Because Saul had been chosen specifically by God to lead and rule the people, he was obligated to obey God in all that he did (1 Samuel 10:25).

Unfortunately, Saul feared the Israelites more than he feared God. He hid in the baggage when Samuel tried to present him as king (1 Samuel 10:20-23), and he blamed other people for his own poor decisions on several occasions (1 Samuel 13:11-12; 14:43-45; 15:20-21, 24, 30). As a result of Saul's weak disobedience, God eventually replaced him with David, a man after God's own heart.

The Ninevites

During Jonah's lifetime, Nineveh was the capital of the ancient empire of Assyria, Israel's most hated and feared enemy. Therefore, it isn't surprising that Jonah initially resisted (and even fled) God's command to go to Nineveh and to warn of impending judgment (Jonah 1:1-3). Jonah was afraid that the hated Ninevites would believe his prophetic warning and repent of their sins (Jonah 4:1-2). Jonah may have also feared what the Ninevites would do to him—a prophet of Israel—for telling them that they were sinfully wrong.

But God was determined that the Ninevites hear the warning, so he saved Jonah from a watery death (Jonah 1:11–2:10) and then sent him to deliver his prophetic message to the Ninevites. When Jonah finally warned the Ninevites of God's coming judgment, the citizens and the king of the city proclaimed a fast—no food or drink—and wore dark, rough cloth instead of their regular clothes. By adopting these ancient mourning practices, the Ninevites intended to demonstrate the genuineness of their prayers of confession and contrition.

All sin is unacceptable to God, so he wants to help us break its hold on our lives. God wants us to repent of our sins. So let's spend a few moments analyzing Psalm 51, David's prayer of repentance after his sin with Bathsheba.

Tell group members they are to read Psalm 51:1-17 together to identify the different components of true repentance. Assign each group one of the following elements:

● what David said about his sin,
● what David committed to do, and
● what David asked God to do.

While groups are working, hang three sheets of newsprint, and label the papers as follows: "What David Said," "What David Will Do," and "What God Will Do."

DEPTHFINDER
UNDERSTANDING REPENTANCE

Biblical repentance differs from modern notions of repentance in several crucial ways. First, biblical repentance is both an attitude and an action. It begins with recognizing your sin and feeling sorry for that sin, but it also involves admitting your sin and committing to change your ways. In addition, biblical repentance involves the entire person, including one's intellect, emotions, and will. The Hebrew and Greek words the Bible uses to describe repentance speak of a "turning" or "changing" of one's mind and life. In short, biblical repentance involves far more than the typical idea of simply feeling sorry for something you have done. To help your kids understand the biblical teaching on repentance, focus on the following elements of true repentance:

● **Admitting we're wrong.** Repentance begins on the intellectual and emotional levels. We must not only recognize that what we have done is sinful in God's eyes but also feel sorry for what we've done. When we view our sinful actions from God's holy perspective, we'll feel sad and remorseful about our sins. This, in turn, will lead us to confess our sins to God and to ask God to forgive them. (See Psalm 51:3-5, 1-2, 6-9.)

● **Committing to change our ways.** Recognizing and confessing our sins is a necessary start, but it's never enough. Biblical repentance also involves an act of the will. We must turn from our sins and commit to God that we will seek to change our ways. We must decide that we will do whatever we can to keep from committing the same sin over and over again. (See Psalm 51:13-15; Jonah 3:8, 10.)

● **Asking God to help us keep our commitment.** None of us have the ability to defeat sin on our own. We need God's help and enabling to overcome sin in our lives. Therefore, when we repent, we need to ask God to give us the power and the perseverance to truly turn from our sins and to develop an obedient character that honors and pleases him. (See Psalm 51:10-15.)

Allow groups several minutes to work, then have them take turns writing on the newsprint and explaining what they discovered. When all the groups have reported, ask the entire group the following questions:

● **What do you think are the basic elements of repentance?**
● **Which of these elements is the most difficult to do? Why?**
● **What will God do for people who genuinely repent of a sin?**
● **How can admitting you're wrong help you change your ways?**
● **What do you think will happen if someone refuses to repent?**
● **Why is it hard to overcome sin when you deny you're wrong?**

Then say: **Psalm 51 shows us that true repentance requires much more than simply saying we're sorry. Genuine repentance involves admitting that we're wrong, committing to change our ways, and asking God to help us follow through with our commitment. Of course, it all begins with admitting that we're wrong because <u>admitting we're wrong helps us change our ways.</u>**

Breaking the Bonds
(up to 10 minutes)
Have kids take out the index cards from the "Sin Safari" activity. Instruct kids to look at their symbols and then discuss the following questions in their small groups:

● **How do you think God feels about your sin? about you?**

● **What do you think God wants you to do about this sin?**

● **Without revealing what sin you're referring to, what makes it hard for you to stop committing this sin?**

● **Think about this question: What will happen if you repent of it? if you don't repent?**

● **How will <u>admitting you're wrong help you change your ways?</u>**

After groups finish answering the questions, ask volunteers to report their groups' responses. Then give each group a marker or a pencil. Tell kids that you'd like them to draw the "No" sign (a circle with a slash through it) over the symbols of their sin while you read from Psalm 51.

Read Psalm 51:1-12, then ask kids to spend one minute in silent prayer, confessing their sins to God and committing themselves to change their ways. After one minute, have group members take turns cutting the ribbon or cloth tying them together. Instruct each student to say, "<u>I've admitted my wrong, and I commit to change my ways</u>" when they cut themselves free.

When everyone has cut the ribbon, have group members conclude by each praying aloud for the person on the right, thanking God for that person's commitment to repent of his or her sin and to live in a way that pleases God.

Encourage kids to take home a strip of ribbon as a reminder of the importance of freeing themselves of sin by admitting they're wrong as the first step in changing their ways.

"Have mercy on me, O God, according to your unfailing love; according to your great compassion blot out my transgressions. Wash away all my iniquity and cleanse me from my sin. For I know my transgressions, and my sin is always before me...Create in me a pure heart, O God, and renew a steadfast spirit within me."

—Psalm 51:1-3, 10

Facts of the Case

You are on trial for a crime you actually committed. Your task is to devise a defense that will convince the judge that you are innocent (or at least that you shouldn't be punished). Read the "facts of the case" below, then work with your group to think up your defense.

The accused

You're a good student and president of the junior class. You carry a B average in school, and you're active in your church youth group. You live with your mother, father, and two younger sisters. Your parents manage a local restaurant together, and they also lead a church Bible study in their spare time.

The charges

You're on trial for vandalizing your high school biology teacher's car.

The evidence

One week prior to the incident, your parents were notified that you were in danger of failing biology. When your parents confronted you with the notice, you lost your temper and claimed that your teacher was "out to get you."

The school janitor claims to have seen you in the vicinity of the car thirty minutes before the damage was discovered.

The car appears to have been struck repeatedly with a tire iron, and your tire iron bears traces of paint that match the color of the car.

Active and Interactive Learning works with teenagers

Let's Start With the Big Picture

Think back to a major life lesson you've learned.

Got it? Now answer these questions:

● Did you learn your lesson from something you read?

● Did you learn it from something you heard?

● Did you learn it from something you experienced?

If you're like 99 percent of your peers, you answered "yes" only to the third question—you learned your life lesson from something you experienced.

This simple test illustrates the most convincing reason for using active and interactive learning with young people: People learn best through experience. Or to put it even more simply, people learn by doing.

Learning by doing is what active learning is all about. No more sitting quietly in chairs and listening to a speaker expound theories about God—that's passive learning. Active learning gets kids out of their chairs and into the experience of life. With active learning, kids get to *do* what they're studying. They *feel* the effects of the principles you teach. They *learn* by experiencing truth firsthand.

Active learning works because it recognizes three basic learning needs and uses them in concert to enable young people to make discoveries on their own and to find practical life applications for the truths they believe.

So what are these three basic learning needs?

1. Teenagers need action.

2. Teenagers need to think.

3. Teenagers need to talk.

Read on to find out exactly how these needs will be met by using the active and interactive learning techniques in Group's Core Belief Bible Study Series in your youth group.

1. Teenagers Need Action

Aircraft pilots know well the difference between passive and active learning. Their passive learning comes through listening to flight instructors and reading flight-instruction books. Their active learning comes through actually flying an airplane or flight simulator. Books and lectures may be helpful, but pilots really learn to fly by manipulating a plane's controls themselves.

We can help young people learn in a similar way. Though we may engage students passively in some reading and listening to teachers, their understanding and application of God's Word will really take off through simulated and real-life experiences.

Forms of active learning include simulation games; role-plays; service projects; experiments; research projects; group pantomimes; mock trials; construction projects; purposeful games; field trips; and, of course, the most powerful form of active learning—real-life experiences.

We can more fully explain active learning by exploring four of its characteristics:

● **Active learning is an adventure.** Passive learning is almost always predictable. Students sit passively while the teacher or speaker follows a planned outline or script.

In active learning, kids may learn lessons the teacher never envisioned. Because the leader trusts students to help create the learning experience, learners may venture into unforeseen discoveries. And often the teacher learns as much as the students.

● **Active learning is fun and captivating.** What are we communicating when we say, "OK, the fun's over—time to talk about God"? What's the hidden message? That joy is separate from God? And that learning is separate from joy?

What a shame.

Active learning is not joyless. One seventh-grader we interviewed clearly remembered her best Sunday school lesson: "Jesus was the light, and we went into a dark room and shut off the lights. We had a candle, and we learned that Jesus is the light and the dark can't shut off the light." That's active learning. Deena enjoyed the lesson. She had fun. And she learned.

Active learning intrigues people. Whether they find a foot-washing experience captivating or maybe a bit uncomfortable, they learn. And they learn on a level deeper than any work sheet or teacher's lecture could ever reach.

● **Active learning involves everyone.** Here the difference between passive and active learning becomes abundantly clear. It's like the difference between watching a football game on television and actually playing in the game.

The "trust walk" provides a good example of involving everyone in active learning. Half of the group members put on blindfolds; the other half serve as guides. The "blind" people trust the guides to lead them through the building or outdoors. The guides prevent the blind people from falling down stairs or tripping over rocks. Everyone needs to participate to learn the inherent lessons of trust, faith, doubt, fear, confidence, and servanthood. Passive spectators of this experience would learn little, but participants learn a great deal.

● **Active learning is focused through debriefing.** Activity simply for activity's sake doesn't usually result in good learning. Debriefing— evaluating an experience by discussing it in pairs or small groups— helps focus the experience and draw out its meaning. Debriefing helps sort and order the information students gather during the experience. It helps learners relate the recently experienced activity to their lives.

The process of debriefing is best started immediately after an experience. We use a three-step process in debriefing: reflection, interpretation, and application.

Reflection—This first step asks the students, "How did you feel?" Active-learning experiences typically evoke an emotional reaction, so it's appropriate to begin debriefing at that level.

Some people ask, "What do feelings have to do with education?" Feelings have everything to do with education. Think back again to that time in your life when you learned a big lesson. In all likelihood, strong feelings accompanied that lesson. Our emotions tend to cement things into our memories.

When you're debriefing, use open-ended questions to probe feelings. Avoid questions that can be answered with a "yes" or "no." Let your learners know that there are no wrong answers to these "feeling" questions. Everyone's feelings are valid.

Interpretation—The next step in the debriefing process asks, "What does this mean to you? How is this experience like or unlike some other aspect of your life?" Now you're asking people to identify a message or principle from the experience.

You want your learners to discover the message for themselves. So instead of telling students your answers, take the time to ask questions that encourage self-discovery. Use Scripture and discussion in pairs or small groups to explore how the actions and effects of the activity might translate to their lives.

Alert! Some of your people may interpret wonderful messages that you never intended. That's not failure! That's the Holy Spirit at work. God allows us to catch different glimpses of his kingdom even when we all look through the same glass.

Application—The final debriefing step asks, "What will you do about it?" This step moves learning into action. Your young people have shared a common experience. They've discovered a principle. Now they must create something new with what they've just experienced and interpreted. They must integrate the message into their lives.

The application stage of debriefing calls for a decision. Ask your students how they'll change, how they'll grow, what they'll do as a result of your time together.

2. Teenagers Need to Think

Today's students have been trained not to think. They aren't dumber than previous generations. We've simply conditioned them not to use their heads.

You see, we've trained our kids to respond with the simplistic answers they think the teacher wants to hear. Fill-in-the-blank student workbooks and teachers who ask dead-end questions such as "What's the capital of Delaware?" have produced kids and adults who have learned not to think.

And it doesn't just happen in junior high or high school. Our children are schooled very early not to think. Teachers attempt to help kids read with nonsensical fill-in-the-blank drills, word scrambles, and missing-letter puzzles.

Helping teenagers think requires a paradigm shift in how we teach. We need to plan for and set aside time for higher-order thinking and be willing to reduce our time spent on lower-order parroting. Group's Core Belief Bible Study Series is designed to help you do just that.

Thinking classrooms look quite different from traditional classrooms. In most church environments, the teacher does most of the talking and hopes that knowledge will transmit from his or her brain to the students'. In thinking settings, the teacher coaches students to ponder, wonder, imagine, and problem-solve.

3. Teenagers Need to Talk

Everyone knows that the person who learns the most in any class is the teacher. Explaining a concept to someone else is usually more helpful to the explainer than to the listener. So why not let the students do more teaching? That's one of the chief benefits of letting kids do the talking. This process is called interactive learning.

What is interactive learning? Interactive learning occurs when students discuss and work cooperatively in pairs or small groups.

Interactive learning encourages learners to work together. It honors the fact that students can learn from one another, not just from the teacher. Students work together in pairs or small groups to accomplish shared goals. They build together, discuss together, and present together. They teach each other and learn from one another. Success as a group is celebrated. Positive interdependence promotes individual and group learning.

Interactive learning not only helps people learn but also helps learners feel better about themselves and get along better with others. It accomplishes these things more effectively than the independent or competitive methods.

Here's a selection of interactive learning techniques that are used in Group's Core Belief Bible Study Series. With any of these models, leaders may assign students to specific partners or small groups. This will maximize cooperation and learning by preventing all the "rowdies" from linking up. And it will allow for new friendships to form outside of established cliques.

Following any period of partner or small-group work, the leader may reconvene the entire class for large-group processing. During this time the teacher may ask for reports or discoveries from individuals or teams. This technique builds in accountability for the teacherless pairs and small groups.

Pair-Share—With this technique each student turns to a partner and responds to a question or problem from the teacher or leader. Every learner responds. There are no passive observers. The teacher may then ask people to share their partners' responses.

Study Partners—Most curricula and most teachers call for Scripture passages to be read to the whole class by one person. One reads; the others doze.

Why not relinquish some teacher control and let partners read and react with each other? They'll all be involved—and will learn more.

Learning Groups—Students work together in small groups to create a model, design artwork, or study a passage or story; then they discuss what they learned through the experience. Each person in the learning group may be assigned a specific role. Here are some examples:

Reader

Recorder (makes notes of key thoughts expressed during the reading or discussion)

Checker (makes sure everyone understands and agrees with answers arrived at by the group)

Encourager (urges silent members to share their thoughts)

When everyone has a specific responsibility, knows what it is, and contributes to a small group, much is accomplished and much is learned.

Summary Partners—One student reads a paragraph, then the partner summarizes the paragraph or interprets its meaning. Partners alternate roles with each paragraph.

The paraphrasing technique also works well in discussions. Anyone who wishes to share a thought must first paraphrase what the previous person said. This sharpens listening skills and demonstrates the power of feedback communication.

Jigsaw—Each person in a small group examines a different concept, Scripture, or part of an issue. Then each teaches the others in the group. Thus, all members teach, and all must learn the others' discoveries. This technique is called a jigsaw because individuals are responsible to their group for different pieces of the puzzle.

JIGSAW EXAMPLE

Here's an example of a jigsaw.

Assign four-person teams. Have teammates each number off from one to four. Have all the Ones go to one corner of the room, all the Twos to another corner, and so on.

Tell team members they're responsible for learning information in their numbered corners and then for teaching their team members when they return to their original teams.

Give the following assignments to various groups:

Ones: Read Psalm 22. Discuss and list the prophecies made about Jesus.

Twos: Read Isaiah 52:13–53:12. Discuss and list the prophecies made about Jesus.

Threes: Read Matthew 27:1-32. Discuss and list the things that happened to Jesus.

Fours: Read Matthew 27:33-66. Discuss and list the things that happened to Jesus.

After the corner groups meet and discuss, instruct all learners to return to their original teams and report what they've learned. Then have each team determine which prophecies about Jesus were fulfilled in the passages from Matthew.

Call on various individuals in each team to report one or two prophecies that were fulfilled.

You Can Do It Too!

All this information may sound revolutionary to you, but it's really not. God has been using active and interactive learning to teach his people for generations. Just look at Abraham and Isaac, Jacob and Esau, Moses and the Israelites, Ruth and Boaz. And then there's Jesus, who used active learning all the time!

Group's Core Belief Bible Study Series makes it easy for you to use active and interactive learning with your group. The active and interactive elements are automatically built in! Just follow the outlines, and watch as your kids grow through experience and positive interaction with others.

FOR DEEPER STUDY

For more information on incorporating active and interactive learning into your work with teenagers, check out these resources:

● *Why Nobody Learns Much of Anything at Church: And How to Fix It,* by Thom and Joani Schultz (Group Publishing) and
● *Do It! Active Learning in Youth Ministry,* by Thom and Joani Schultz (Group Publishing).

your evaluation of

Bible Study Series
for senior high

why FORGIVENESS matters

Group Publishing, Inc.
Attention: Core Belief Talk-Back
P.O. Box 481
Loveland, CO 80539
Fax: (970) 669-1994

Please help us continue to provide innovative and useful resources for ministry. After you've led the studies in this volume, take a moment to fill out this evaluation; then mail or fax it to us at the address above. Thanks!

● ● ● ● ● ●

1. As a whole, this book has been (circle one)

not very helpful   very helpful
1   2   3   4   5   6   7   8   9   10

2. The best things about this book:

3. How this book could be improved:

4. What I will change because of this book:

5. Would you be interested in field-testing future Core Belief Bible Studies and giving us your feedback? If so, please complete the information below:

Name _____

Street address _____

City _____ State _____Zip _____

Daytime telephone (____) _____ Date _____

THANKS!